better together*

*This book is best read together, grownup and kid.

 akidsco.com

a
kids
book
about

a kids book about

BEING

TRANSGENDER

by Gia Parr
in partnership with *The GenderCool Project*

A Kids Co.
Editor Denise Morales Soto
Designers Duke Stebbins and Rick DeLucco
Creative Director Rick DeLucco
Studio Manager Kenya Feldes
Sales Director Melanie Wilkins
Head of Books Jennifer Goldstein
CEO and Founder Jelani Memory

DK
Editor Emma Roberts
Senior Production Editor Jennifer Murray
Senior Production Controller Louise Minihane
Senior Acquisitions Editor Katy Flint
Acquisitions Project Editor Sara Forster
Managing Art Editor Vicky Short
Publishing Director Mark Searle
DK would like to thank Ellen Jones

This American Edition, 2024
Published in the United States by DK Publishing
1745 Broadway, 20th Floor, New York, NY 10019

DK, a Division of Penguin Random House LLC

A catalog record for this book is available from the Library of Congress.
ISBN: 978-0-7440-9473-2

DK books are available at special discounts when purchased in bulk for
sales promotions, premiums, fund-raising, or educational use. For details, contact:
DK Publishing Special Markets, 1745 Broadway, 20th Floor, New York, NY 10019, or SpecialSales@dk.com

Printed and bound in China

www.dk.com

akidsco.com

To every kiddo out there who is living
the life they were always meant to live,
and to the grownups who believe in them.

To all our GenderCool Champion friends
whose voices helped make this book a reality.
We are changing the world: Alex, Ashton, Chazzie,
Daniel, Eve, Greyson, Hunter, Jonathan, Kai, Landon,
Lia, Max, Rose, Rebekah, Sivan, Stella, and Tru.

Intro
for grownups

Transgender kids are real. They are creative, joyous, and a handful—just like any other kids! There are hundreds of thousands of kids who are transgender in the US, and they belong to every community and come from all different backgrounds. Just like anyone else, they need the love and support of the grownups in their lives in order to thrive.

Maybe you're reading this book because it's time to have a discussion. Time to learn. Time to shake off whatever confusion, skepticism, concern, or biases you may have. Look, we get it. Until you actually meet or raise a transgender kid, the whole thing might seem out of reach. We hope this book and Gia's story will change that. While everyone's journey to understanding their gender is unique to them, we hope Gia's experience makes it easier to understand those who experience something similar.

And if you've landed here because you do have a personal connection to a transgender person, then congratulations! You are incredibly lucky.

—The GenderCool Team

HEY!

I'm Gia.

I use she/her pronouns* and my favorite food is ice cream!

Something cool about me is that I am *transgender*.

Have you ever heard
the word *transgender* before?

Do you know what it means?

It's OK if you don't!
Let me try to explain.

When you're born,
a doctor looks at you and says,

"It's a boy!"

or,

"It's a girl!"

based on your body.

From then on, you are expected to act a certain way based on what the doctor said.*

But that's not the whole picture.

*This is what we call gender roles.

Sometimes who we actually are is different

from what
people think.

You see, when I was born,
the doctor said,

"It's a boy!"

But...

I always knew

this wasn't true.

I loved playing with dolls and dressing up like a princess.

I would put a T-shirt on my head and pretend I had long hair.

I even had purple pants that I refused to take off.

All these things made me feel like me.*

And who people saw me as
didn't feel like me at all.

I remember one time,
our teacher asked our class
to draw self-portraits
as an assignment.

I picked up my crayons
and a piece of paper and
started drawing a boy
with short curly hair.

But as I was drawing,
it didn't feel right.

Because *I knew that wasn't me*.

So, I started

over.

I grabbed a new piece of paper and I drew who I know I am on the inside:

a girl with long hair and a flowy dress.

But my classmates saw me
as a boy and were confused
by my portrait.

Because it didn't match
what they saw, even though
it was exactly how I saw myself.

This scared me.
So I hid who I was.

For those of you who are reading this and don't know what hiding your identity* feels like...

*Our identity is how each of us identifies who we are, to ourselves and to others.

Picture a room with
4 walls and a door.

This room is decorated
however you like.

The walls are whatever
color you want them to be.
So are the curtains,
and the rug.

It's filled with all the things
that make you happy
on the inside.

But you have to
stay in that room.

You aren't allowed to come out or let anyone in.

This is how I felt.

The world saw me one way...

while my identity was trapped in a room.

One day,
I decided to donate
almost all my dolls, toys,
and princess dresses.

Whatever I had left
was put in my room
where only I could see.

> *I put all of me in one small space.*

I shut my door and didn't let anyone in.

No one knew the real me. I felt alone, sad, and lost

Years passed, and I still felt lost.

I wondered, *Why am I like this?*

One day, I looked up

"boy who feels like girl"

online and found stories of people who were just like me.

That was the first time I heard
the word *transgender*.

I realized I wasn't alone.

The feeling I had of being a girl
finally made sense.

I was still afraid to share who I truly was, but the longer I stayed trapped in my room, the smaller and smaller it became.

I felt like I had no choice.

So, one night, I wrote a note to my parents telling them who I was, and slipped it under their bedroom door.

After they read it,
they walked out,
pulled me into a hug, and
told me they believed
me and that they loved me.

After that,

my door slowly started opening.

**From that day on,
I was done hiding.**

Being open was what made me happy.

So, before I started 8th grade, my family sent a letter to my middle school telling them who I really am.

On the first day of school,
I walked out of my room,
and this time,

I left the door wide open.

The sad little boy who had
walked into that room years ago

...proudly came out as Gia.

Now I feel like me, buying the clothes I want.

Now I feel like me, hanging out with my friends and sitting with them at lunch.

Now I feel like me, growing out my hair.

Now I feel like me, wearing makeup.

Now I feel like me, using she/her pronouns.

These are some parts of
what is known as *transition*.

They may seem like small things, or things you never really think about,* but they matter in **BIG** ways.

*Or maybe you think about them all the time.

Because
they make us
who we are.

It may be really hard or scary to let people in, but if you do, you will always find people who love you exactly as you are.

Now, everyone is welcome in my room.

Now, I am me.

I am Gia.

Outro
for grownups

Now that you've gotten to know Gia, where can you go from here? Maybe you know someone who just shared who they truly are with you. How would you respond?

Believe them. Most children have a strong sense of their gender identity as early as 4 years old, so believe them when they tell you who they are and watch them thrive.

Choose positivity. We have a conscious choice regarding how we respond, so celebrate them and stay focused on what's really important!

Give people the chance to understand. A wise parent once said, "Put awesome out there, and chances are, you'll get awesome back."

Embrace change. Learning that someone you love is transgender is definitely a change for you and a cause for celebration for them! It's OK that things turned out differently than how you imagined, but we encourage you to run toward that change. It will invigorate you.

—The GenderCool Team

About The Author

Gia Parr (she/her) is a 20-year-old college student and presidential scholar studying communications. She was a high school senior when she wrote this book. She is passionate about advocacy, school, modeling, and acting. From being a part of major brand campaigns to speaking to thousands of business leaders, Gia uses her platform to progress the rights of all communities.

Gia helped launch and now serves on the Board of Directors of The GenderCool Project, a youth-led movement replacing misinformed opinions with positive experiences meeting transgender and nonbinary youth who are thriving. Through education, advocacy, leadership development, and visibility, GenderCool is uniquely impacting culture, policy, and business worldwide. Learn more at GenderCool.org.

 @gendercool    @gendercool    www.gendercool.org

Made to empower.

a kids book about racism
by Jelani Memory

a kids book about ANXIETY
by Ross Szabo

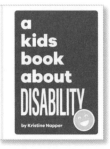
a kids book about DISABILITY
by Kristine Napper

a kids book about IMAGINATION
by LEVAR BURTON

a kids book about belonging
by Kevin Carroll

a kids book about failyure
by Dr. Laymon Hicks

a kids book about GRATITUDE
by Ben Kenyon

a kids book about LIFE ONLINE
by Dave S. Anderson & Blake Fleischacker

a kids book about body image
by Rebecca Alexander

a kids book about IMMIGRATION
by MJ Calderon

a kids book about EMPATHY
by Daron K. Roberts

a kids book about GENDER
by Dale Mueller

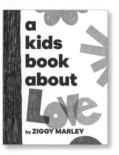
a kids book about Love
by ZIGGY MARLEY

a kids book about EQUALITY
by BILLIE JEAN KING

a kids book about MONEY
by Adam Stramwasser

a kids book about FEMINISM
by Emma McIlroy

a kids book about adventure
by Dr. Ben Tertin

a kids book about CLIMATE CHANGE
by Zanagee Artis & Olivia Greenspan

a kids book about CONFIDENCE
by Joy Cho

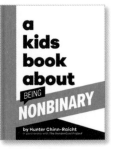
a kids book about BEING NONBINARY
by Hunter Chinn-Raicht
in partnership with The GenderCool Project

Discover more at akidsco.com